where my story begins

rachel longhurst  krystin longhurst

designed by
andrea robbins

R.A.K. Publishing

We would like to express our graditude to family and friends

who shared their words of wisdom along our journey.

Copyright ©2005
by Rachel Longhurst
All rights reserved.
First Edition, 2005
Library of Congress Control Number: 2005902517
ISBN 0-9767354-0-7

R.A.K. Publishing
220 West Lafayette
Milford, MI 48381
248✎685✎8528
wheremystorybegins@comcast.net

Without the hard work, dedication and creativity of
Andrea Robbins, our story could not have been told. She captured
what was held in our hearts and brought it to life on paper.
Her support throughout this process was enormous and
for that we will be eternally grateful!

A heart felt hug and thank you goes to our family,
whose love and dedication to our animals
shape and mold them into the wonderful characters they become.

IT WAS LOVE AT FIRST SIGHT!

They were captivated by my
enormous, clumsy paws
and my piles of wrinkly puppy skin.
What won them over
was my whimsical expression that would melt
even the toughest of hearts.
They knew I was the one who would become a
new member of their family.
They had fallen in **LOVE!**

I'm a Labrador Retriever.
We come in three different colors,
black,
chocolate
and **ME!**
I'm a Yellow Lab.
I was born January 10, 1996.

Choosing the right name for me
took a great deal of thought.
Mom wanted me to be called **NORMAN**,
but Dad, Brother and Sis said, "**NO WAY!**"
They agreed **COREY** was a perfect name
for a special puppy like me!

My buddy Lucas, is a Golden Retriever.
I couldn't have asked for a better **COMPANION!**
Lucas is the one I look up to.
He has shown me the ropes.
I stand next to him when my confidence wanders
and feel strong and safe.
I **LOVE** him with all my heart!

WHAT A PAL!

Everyday I have a few chores to do.
My dad is up early for work, so one way I help
out is to run outside and bring in the morning
newspaper. Even before the sun rises,
or when it's raining or snowing

🦴 I DO IT! 🦴

It's just one of those things expected of me.
Dad is always so grateful for my help.
He treats me with a snack and a soft pat on the
head for a job well done.
Having a job makes me feel **IMPORTANT**.
I'm glad I can help out!

I also have to be on guard in our backyard.
My family loves to feed the birds,
but the silly squirrels try to steal their food.
Well... that's where I come in.
I let the squirrels play and eat for a little while,
but when I decide their time is up,
off I run and chase them away.

I DO GOOD WORK!

I love to exercise.
It keeps my muscles **STRONG!**
Many mornings after retrieving the newspaper,
Mom, Lucas and I go for a walk through town.
We see kids waiting for the school bus
and I always stop to wag hello!
It puts smiles on their faces
and giggles in my wiggle.

And oh, the smells from the bakery!
They fill the air
and make my belly rumble for breakfast.
Lucas is always hopeful someone will share
a bite of doughnut with him!

We see the sun wake up
smiling it's brilliant pinks
and yellows all around us.
Sometimes, the geese fly overhead
and honk out a "**GOOD MORNING**" greeting.
The church bells ring
and fill the morning air with music.

It all makes me feel **SPECIAL**,
so I move a little faster
and wag my tail
to the rhythm of the morning.

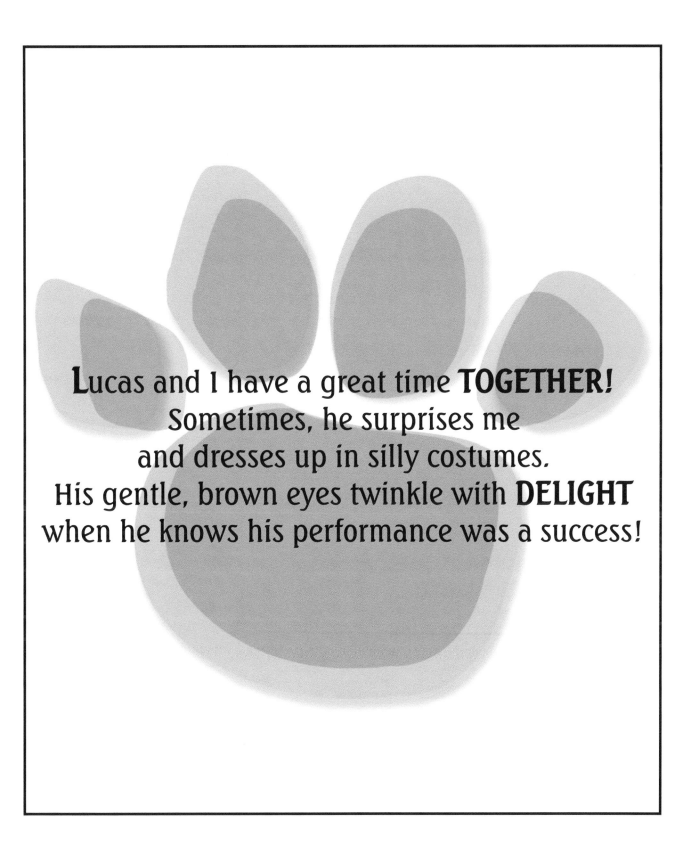

Lucas and I have a great time **TOGETHER!**
Sometimes, he surprises me
and dresses up in silly costumes.
His gentle, brown eyes twinkle with **DELIGHT**
when he knows his performance was a success!

Other times,
we wrestle or play tag,
but our favorite game is tug-of-war.
Once in a while,
I grab hold of Lucas' ear by mistake.
He doesn't minds though,
because he knows I'm only playing
and would never hurt him.

HE'S MY BEST FRIEND!

Lucas reminds me of Grandpa,
because he's older than me.
After we play I let him rest, but
I'm so full of energy it's often hard to do.
I dig deep to find my
PATIENCE
and wait for him to wake up.

Lucas and I love to sink our paws into a
cool lake on a **HOT** summer day.
My family will throw a favorite toy
or a stick for me to fetch.
I'll get a **RUNNING START,**
take a **GIANT LEAP**
and **SPLASH**
into the water and retrieve my prize.

THAT'S WHAT RETRIEVERS DO!

When fetching objects too big for just one dog, Lucas and I must work together.

BEST BUDDIES
MAKE AN AMAZING TEAM!

Have **YOU** ever played in the water?
Maybe tried to catch some frogs
or hunt for seashells?
Me, I just love to be **WET!**
Not just a little **WET**,
but an all over soaking **WET!**
I can entertain myself for hours
digging holes in the sand
in search of buried treasures.
On one adventure, I uncovered
three smooth, shimmering rocks.
I ran to shore carrying
my riches in my mouth
so I could reveal them to my family.
They were so **PROUD** of my discovery!

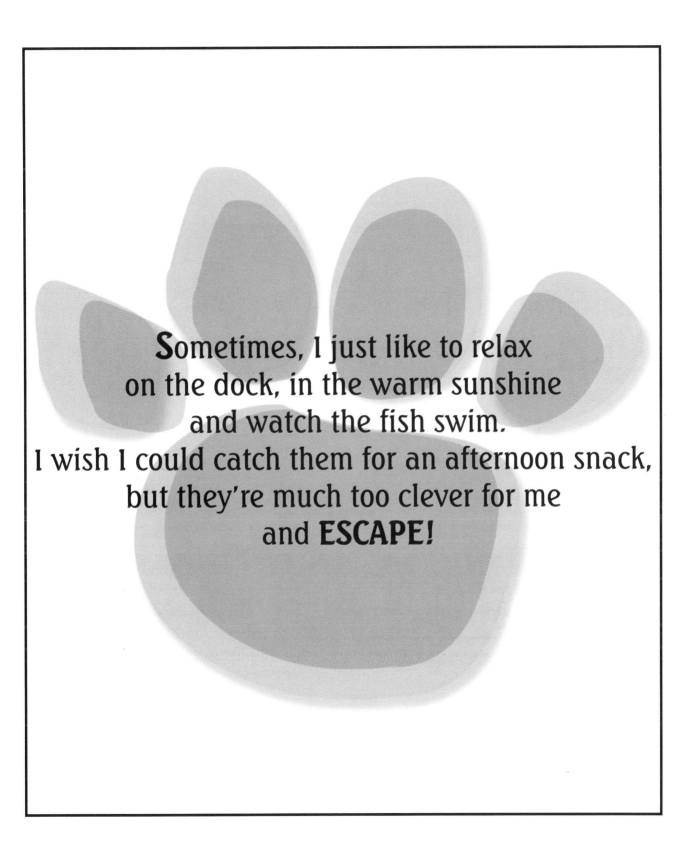

Sometimes, I just like to relax
on the dock, in the warm sunshine
and watch the fish swim.
I wish I could catch them for an afternoon snack,
but they're much too clever for me
and **ESCAPE!**

I love to go on rides,
whether it's in a car, a boat ...

...or just a simple wheel barrel ride
in our backyard!
I'll jump into the co-pilot seat
faster than you can imagine!
I love the feel of my ears **FLAPPING** in the wind
while my nose **BREATHES** in the fresh air.
My voice **YELPS** out my joy and excitement
as I anxiously await
the destination of our journey.

I have so many favorite things,
but my all time favorite is....
... carrying my dish in my mouth.
When I wake up, I run around the house...
...carrying my dish in my mouth.
When people come to visit, I greet them...
...carrying my dish in my mouth.
When I'm out in the yard,
I'm as proud as can be...
...carrying my dish in my mouth.
But, the best time
is when I have to take my dish out of my mouth
and my family fills it with food.
DINNER!
 **YUM**
THAT'S MY FAVORITE TIME OF DAY!

There are times when I just love to be **QUIET**.
I lay down and think about
all the **FUN** I have had,
all the squirrels I have **CHASED**,
all the rides I have **TAKEN**,
all the newspapers I have **FETCHED**,
all the sticks I have **RETRIEVED**,
all the ropes I have **TUGGED**,
all the fields I have **EXPLORED**,
all the waters I have **WADED**,
all the treasures I have **DISCOVERED**,
all the goodies I have **EATEN**,
all the lives I have **TOUCHED**,
all the moments I have spent with **MY FAMILY**.
Most of all, I think about
what a **LUCKY** dog I am!

🦴 01/10/96 ~ 05/20/04 🦴

~Where My Story Ends~

This book is dedicated to a very special Yellow Lab,
COREY,
who touched our lives in so many ways.
His spirit for life was contagious!
Every morning we awoke to his enthusiasm.
How excited he was to always bring in the morning paper
and anxiously demand breakfast,
acting as though he hadn't eaten for weeks.
Then, proudly carry his dish around showing his gratitude.
He was an incredible athlete!
What a joy it was to take him for long walks
and to let him run through open fields and wooded areas.
He would leap and soar as though he had wings.
Now he will fly with the angels in heaven.
-How we would love to visit-
After those runs he loved to snuggle, as close as possible,
while he regained his energy for the next time.
We desperately miss the comfort of his touch, his warmth,
as he would curl up between us in bed.
He cherished people large and small, especially
his buddy Lucas, a Golden Retriever.
He holds such a special place in our hearts.
Corey was taken from us much too soon because of an illness.
Words cannot express how deeply he is missed.

**May you all enjoy, love and cherish your puppies
unconditionally as they do us!**